SUPPLEMENT TO

Volume 1:

WEST GLOUCESTER & WYE VALLEY LINES

INTRODUCTION

With some important new colour images having come to light in the five years since *West Gloucester & Wye Valley Lines* was first published, it was felt that the time was right for an enlarged new edition. However, after sampling a reasonably large cross section of those in the Wye Valley area who already own a first edition and thus would not wish to buy the whole book again, I took the view that it was only fair to issue the additional forty-eight pages as this separate supplement as well.

Many of the new pictures fill what I felt were significant gaps in the original coverage and I have thus endeavoured to place them through the main book in both context and order. I have also then carried through that aim here, so the journey followed mirrors that of the book, starting at Gloucester and visiting the Llanthony Docks Branch, the Ledbury Branch, the line to Ross and Hereford and the Wye Valley branches, before heading back up

the main line from Chepstow past the Severn Bridge and through Newnham. There are some veritable gems here and I believe the overall coverage is good enough that this slim volume stands on its own merits. The Walford Halt picture was swapped in the main book, for the better view to be found on the rear cover here, whilst repeated on the inside covers are three pictures which were miss-identified in the first edition, now with their corrected locations. Gaps still remain to be filled, with colour views of the halts at Backney, Malswick and Westbury-on-Severn yet to be found, along with the stations at Woolaston (closed in 1954) and Tidenham, and the junction at Rotherwas.

Acknowledgements are due to Roy Denison, Alan Jarvis, John Jenkins, Don Mann, Brian Mills, John Ryan, Tim Stephens and Chris Walker; also to Paul Chancellor at Colour-Rail and to Macolm Bobbitt and John Dagley-Morris. *Neil Parkhouse, Lydney, 2018*

The 13.25pm from Hereford to Gloucester heads away from Weston-under-Penyard behind No. 4157 on 15th August 1964. This is the best detail colour view seen to date of the basic facilities provided here and shows the non-standard colour which the hut and nameboard support posts were painted latterly. Note the temporary speed restriction signal on the left; presumably work was being carried out on the line a short distance further on. JOHN RYAN

A fine view beneath the canopy on Gloucester Central's Platform 1, looking west towards Hereford and South Wales during a quiet period on Monday 7th June 1965. With the closure from early November 1964 of the line to Hereford, the Sharpness Branch, many of the local stations on the main lines radiating out from Gloucester and the cessation of the Chalford auto trains, the station lost much of the hustle and bustle evident from earlier pictures. The diesel shunter just visible in the centre distance was a harbinger of the future, with the end of steam just over six months away. The array of hanging enamelled signs, for the various rooms and offices, lead down to the entrance/exit just before the bookstall. The soulless mid-1970s rebuilding of the station moved the main entrance on to the platform nearer to where the photographer was standing. ROY DENISON

ABOVE: Collett 0-6-0 No. 2241, in WR lined green passenger livery, blows off gently in the bay platform whilst waiting to depart with a train for Hereford in the summer of 1962. A lengthy allocation to Hereford shed (86C), from May 1958 to withdrawal in February 1964, was interrrupted by a brief sojourn down to Exmouth Junction in the late summer of 1963. Note the Parcels Train Brake Van on the left, lettered for 'WOLVERHAMPTON SWINDON AND SWANSEA'. ALAN JARVIS

BELOW: Consecutively numbered Collett No. 2242, also of Hereford shed and again wearing lined green, has just been given the right away with another Ross line train but this time departing from the main platform in 1962. New in April 1945, No. 2242's time at Hereford lasted from July 1957 to early November 1964, when it was transferred to Horton Road for its final six months of service. ALAN JARVIS

RIGHT: The east end of the station, with a rake of 'Herring' hoppers loaded with ballast stone from Whitecliff Quarry near Coleford in the Forest of Dean, standing on the Up main line circa 1963. The grey painted 'Shark' brake van bringing up the rear was lettered 'C.O. RETURN TO LYDNEY. W.R.'. NPC

BELOW: The Berry Wiggins tank wagon at the head of this freight marks it as another from the Forest of Dean, off the Cinderford Branch. Class '57XX' No. 4689 had been allocated to Horton Road shed in March 1965, which would thus date this view as the summer of that year. NPC

LEFT: BR 'Standard' Class '5' 4-6-0s were not common motive power on Hereford line services, so this view of No. 73070 waiting to depart from the bay on 31st August 1964 merits inclusion on that basis alone. No. 73070 came new from Crewe Works in November 1954 and was based at Shrewsbury at the time of this picture, so was being worked back home via Hereford. It was withdrawn from Bolton shed in April 1967. The two boys, 6-year old Eric and 8-year old John Jenkins were about to enjoy a ride over the line in the company of their father, holding the camera. John, in the red pullover, went on to enjoy a 43-year career on the railway, starting as a Signal Engineer Trainee at Gloucester in 1972 and ending in 2015 as Principal Assistant to the Western Route Signal Engineer, specialising in manual signalling and level crossing control systems.
G.H.C. JENKINS, COURTESY JOHN JENKINS

ABOVE: A Collett 0-6-0 heads towards Gloucester with a pick-up goods from Hereford on 3rd February 1961. The train is on the low embankment passing the Little Meadow playing fields, leading from the brick arches of St. Catherine's Viaduct in the middle distance. Beyond that can just be seen Black Bridge (the OS refers to it as Pump House Bridge) over the East Channel of the River Severn, which had been rebuilt as a single span by British Railways in 1957. This replaced the original 125ft long, iron swing bridge designed by Brunel, the Gloucester & Dean Forest Railway which built this section of line being required by its Act to keep the channel clear for the passage of sailing vessels. To its left can also be seen the brick-built pump house for the pumping engines that operated the bridge, which swung on a central pier. The pump house still stands, albeit now in a derelict state. ROY DENISON

RIGHT: Gloucester Horton Road shed's Collett 0-6-0 No. 3203 pilots an unidentified 'Large Prairie' heading west away from Gloucester and just coming off Black Bridge, circa 1963. No details were recorded by the photographer, so we don't know whether this is a train for Hereford or a Cardiff 'stopper'. CHRIS WALKER

On 10th August 1963, an unidentified ex-GWR 'Mogul' is seen at the start of its journey to Hereford with a Saturday service loaded to four coaches. Just visible in the left distance above the roof of the rear carriage is Ham Viaduct, similar in design to St Catherine's Viaduct and in common with that structure provided to assist the passage of flood water, the fields here being part of the Gloucester flood plain. The blue brick arches in the foreground performed a similar task but were not of a sufficient size to be graced with a name. The cathedral provides a prominent landmark in the central background and on the right can be seen the Over Causeway, a road thought originally to date back to the Romans, which is now a dual carriageway. Given the propensity of this area for flooding, it seems almost incredible to note that an electricity sub-station was built near here, on a site just to the north of the railway in the left distance. After a major flooding scare in 2007, millions of pounds then had to be spent building new flood barriers around it. NPC

A rake of vans trundles away from Llanthony Sidings behind one of the Class '03' diesel shunters circa 1964. In the background, a line-up of eleven withdrawn ex-GWR engines, mostly tender types but with a couple of 'Prairie' 2-6-2 tanks at the nearer end and a pannier tank tucked in towards the far end, are stored awaiting their final journey to one of the South Wales scrapyards. This is clearly a different batch to those photographed by Bill Potter. Whilst most of them are likely to have been withdrawn from Horton Road shed, that may not have been the case for all of them and they may have been stored here for some months, to give time for bids from scrap merchants to be sought and evaluated. Barnwood shed, closed in May 1963, was also used for storage of withdrawn engines. Opposite them, a rake of steel mineral wagons can be seen at the end of the Castle Meads power station branch. NPC

A very late candidate for inclusion in these additional pages was this view of Class '57XX' No. 4698 heading on to the Llanthony Docks Branch at Over with a pick-up freight from the Forest of Dean Branch on 6th August 1965; the view also most likely dates the picture of the same engine entering Gloucester on page 5. As with that picture, No. 4698 displays another chalked 'LINER' inscription on this side but I have no idea what it means. Almost the full expanse of Over Sidings can be discerned in the background, leading down to the water tower just visible above the 0-6-0PT's cab roof. DON MANN

ABOVE: An unusual aspect of Over Junction Signal Box, taken from the A40 road overbridge on 16th July 1964, six weeks after the line had closed, and looking towards Gloucester. Nearer to the camera is the base of the earlier Over Junction Signal Box, built by Mackenzie & Holland circa 1884 and extended in 1903. The main line had run just in front of this box up until its realignment to riun over a new bridge over the River Severn in 1957. In the right background is the now closed Port Ham electricity sub-station, which was connected to Castlemeads Power Station. BRIAN MILLS

LEFT: A close-up of the Up starter for the Ledbury Branch, which had a subsidiary 'Calling-On' arm below, along with detail of the A40 overbridge, built of Forest of Dean red sandstone with a wrought iron span. The polished rails were from the demolition trains, as dismantling of the line was in process. BRIAN MILLS

BELOW: Looking north from the A40 bridge, showing the start of the single line. BRIAN MILLS

A rare colour view of trains crossing at Newent, as railcar No. W19W waits for Collett 0-6-0 No. 2207 to arrive with the branch pick-up goods on 10th July 1959. New in August 1939, the '22XX' was at Kidderminster shed from 1953, transferring to Gloucester Horton Road in March 1956, where it spent the rest of its relatively short career, withdrawal taking place in January 1961. Being a single track branch, the driver of the railcar will exchange the staff for the Dymock to Newent section with the token for the Newent to Over Junction section, about to be handed over by the fireman of No. 2207. Once the railcar has departed, the 0-6-0 will then be free to shunt the yard here, before carrying on northwards to Dymock and Ledbury. Was No. 2207 a new 'cop' for the schoolboy spotter on his bike on the left? This is another slide, bought off an internet auction site, which came with no recorded provenance, so sadly the identity of the photographer is not known to me. NPC

RIGHT: Another study of No. 78001 at Newent on 16th may 1964, on what would have been a very relaxed day out for the crew. They would have been aware that the end was near, so there were not many occasions left on which to enjoy rosters such as this. Although the official final closure date was given as 1st June, the last trip up the branch, by No. 78001 and a brake van to collect any remaining empty wagons, took place on Saturday 30th May. NPC

LEFT: A final brief return to better days at Newent, in this busy scene from the late 1950s. A large and varied selection of parcels and sacks can be seen on the platform, that have either just been unloaded from railcar W19W or are about to be placed on board. Is that also a goose nonchalantly wandering around? The picture gives an indication of the lifeline that the railway still provided for this small country town in north west Gloucestershire, a service, however, which would soon be taken over by road transport. COLOUR-RAIL

RIGHT: The closed single line at Four Oaks Halt on 16th July 1964, photographed from the same overbridge. The track, still in pristine condition, was bullhead rail on concrete sleepers, whilst the telegraph rig was also in excellent condition–clearly quite a recent replacement although the wires had been removed. The M50 motorway overbridge can be seen nearing completion in the distance. Note that although two years had elapsed since the previous picture was taken, the halt nameboard was still lying on the platform at the base of the lamppost. BRIAN MILLS

A half a mile west of Over there is a major road junction where the A48 commences, branching off south-westwards away from the A40 towards Lydney, Chepstow and South Wales. Some 119 miles later, after following the curve of the South Wales coastline through Cardiff and Swansea, the A48 joins up with the A40 again at Carmarthen. This view of Class 9F No. 92215 heading towards South Wales with a load of iron ore was taken from the verge of the A48 near its start and close to the bridge carrying it over the line. It is undated but the engine was allocated to Banbury shed until early September 1963, so the picture is likely to be a few weeks prior to that. Upper Moorcroft Farm features in the right background. NPC

From a similar vantage point, Class '22XX' No. 2242 made for a pretty picture as it hurried by with the 12.25pm from Gloucester to Hereford on 9th May 1964. As a resident of Hereford shed since July 1957, it no doubt had come to know the route well but No. 2242 was transferred to Horton Road in November 1964 after the line was closed, where it lasted just six more months, being withdrawn in May 1965, the wholesale closure of Gloucestershire branch and secondary lines having left many of these smaller engines with little or no work. Whilst the A48 bridge has been heavily rebuilt with a massive concrete parapet which blocks all views of the railway, a photograph taken from this exact spot today will show little change apart from the loss of the telegraph pole route. NPC

No. 6318 gathers speed as it leaves Oakle Street station for the final time on Saturday 31st October 1964, the final day of train services between Gloucester and Hereford, although the official closure date was Monday 2nd November. This happened on many lines which did not have a Sunday service but those on the Ross line did not run on the final Sunday. John Strange, who also took a shot here but a few seconds earlier, will be one of the little group of photographers in the left distance. ROY DENISON

A delightful study of the small wayside station at Oakle Street, basking in late autumn sunshine on 3rd November 1962 and showing the simple wooden buildings provided here. This sleepy halt served a small hamlet of just a few scattered cottages and farms, as well as the more distant but larger village of Minsterworth, spread out along nearly a mile of the parallel A48. Despite being on the main line, it had only a limited time table, being served by Gloucester-Hereford trains only, not those heading to and from South Wales. The station opened for passengers on 9th September 1851 but then did not appear in the timetables between 1856 and 1870. The signal box, which had been sited on the far end of the Down platform, was closed circa 1953-4, the siding and goods bay on the left then being accessed by a ground frame. The goods yard was closed on 12th August 1963, with the siding and ground frame being taken out on 13th October. Note the colour light signal opposite on the Down side. There were two minor level crossings on the short section ahead to Grange Court Junction, at Ley Road (just discernible in the distance) and Frowen's Lane, both of which are still in operation today, although the latter appears to be only a farm track and is very restricted use. ROY DENISON

A closer view of the main buildings, on the Up side and looking towards Gloucester on its last day. The nearer timber building was originally all the accommodation that was provided here. The brick building and gents urinal were later additions, probably in the 1890s but certainly by 1902, along with the brick shelter on the Down side; this originally had a small canopy but no such luxury was ever provided for the main building. Note the faded nameboard set back by the fence on the left, whilst although the ground frame and yard had been taken out a year earlier, little effort seems to have been made to remove the materials and equipment from the site. The only reminder of the station's existence today is the station master's house, the lofty red brick building visible in the centre background. ROY DENISON

Whilst graced by few passengers, Grange Court Junction must have been a wonderful location to watch and photograph the plethora of passing trains. Here, on a summer's day circa 1964, an unidentified but heavily work-stained '9F' 2-10-0 rumbles through on the Down main line with a lengthy mixed freight bound for South Wales. The locomotive's smokebox numberplate is almost decipherable and it might be No. 72070, which between June 1963 and March 1965 was a Leicester Midland based engine. NPC

Whilst the number of wonderful additional colour transparencies that have turned up since this volume was first published undoubtedly justifies this supplement, my personal favourite amongst all of them is unquestionably this hugely nostalgic and rare view of the road approach to Grange Court station, surrounded by mature pine trees and beautifully lit by shafts of sunlight. Anonymous and undated, it was probably taken in 1964, a few months before closure. Coincidentally, within a short space of time I also acquired a superb black and white negative of almost the same view but taken in the mid 1950s. Nothing remains of these magnificent red sandstone buildings today, so this image serves to remind us what another architectural gem we have lost. Did the bicycle belong to the photographer? NPC

RIGHT: Trains on the route from Hereford could cross at numerous places, including here at Grange Court Junction, where single line working either started or finished depending on the direction of travel. No. 4161 draws its train away from the Up branch platform, having crossed a corresponding Down service in the station behind. The bare ballast in the foreground following the removal of the sidings indicate a summer 1964 date and probably on a Saturday given No. 4161's load of four coaches plus van. NPC

BELOW: The fireman on this Collett 0-6-0 heading to Hereford leans out to collect the single line token from the apparatus opposite the 60-lever signal box. The catcher can be seen on the other side of the line. These saved the signalman a walk along the platform at this busy box but to save even having to walk down the steps, they often used a pole with a hook, which they dangled out of the window to collect the token from the fireman. NPC

The service withdrawal notice in one of the waiting rooms at Grange Court. NPC

A circa 1964 close-up of the Up side branch platform waiting room at Grange Court, which was in the same style and construction as the rest of the station. It was also provided with a gents toilets, at the far end. NPC

More detail of the station buildings, showing the exposed nature of the island platform shelter, which although stylish offered little protection from the elements. In terms of passenger numbers, Grange Court was never a busy station and by the final decade this deserted scene would have been typical. It served the small village of Northwood Green just to the north-west of the line but took its name from the court and farm immediately to the south-east of the station. Apart from the sparsely populated local area, anyone travelling from stations on the Hereford line could also change trains here to head south and *vice versa* but this never amounted to any significant total either. The closure of the Hereford line was thus to sound its death knell, there being little reason to retain the station afterwards and, along with Oakle Street and Newnham, it was closed. Other intermediate stops between Gloucester and Lydney, at Westbury-on-Severn and Awre, had already gone, leaving this 22 mile section with no intermediate station, as it remains today. NPC

Another of Roy Denison's superb station studies, showing the full layout at Blaisdon on 12th August 1962, over a year before the goods yard was removed, although the rust on the rails would suggest that it had not seen any traffic for some months at least prior to this view. Pre-dating the establishment of the halt, Blaisdon Siding was opened for goods traffic on 12th November 1906 and, as seen here, comprised a loop with two short stubs at either end, one of which ran alongside the dock holding the livestock pen in the left foreground. The siding was officially taken out of use on 11th October 1963 and removed the following month. Traffic to and from it would had been largely agricultural in nature, no doubt including consignments of Blaisdon plums when in season, plus consignments of house coal coming inwards. Roy DENISON

Photographer John Ryan had just alighted from the departing Gloucester-bound train on Saturday 15th August 1964, so he could photograph Blaisdon Halt. The service comprised eleven trains each way on a Saturday, so his wait for the next Down train was probably around an hour. JOHN RYAN

Looking the opposite way from the embankment leading up to the road overbridge almost exactly a year earlier, No. 6365 drifts towards the halt with an Up train on 10th August 1963. Up on the hillside on the right is Blaisdon Hall, built in 1876 by South Wales and Forest of Dean iron master William Crawshay for his son Edwin. In 1935 it was bought by the Silesian Society and used as an agricultural school for training underpriviliged boys. It is now an upmarket wedding venue. NPC

In common with '5101' classmate No. 4161, No. 4157 was latterly another regular on the line between Gloucester and Hereford. The picture is undated but the locomotive had been transferred to Hereford from Pontypool Road in June 1964, so it must have been taken in the summer of that year. The location was also not given but I am fairly certain that is on the line just to the west of Blaisdon Halt, as it approaches Blaisdon Woods (with No. 4157 thus bound for Hereford). The road overbridge just visible in the background and the pole route being to the left (or north) of the line at this point pretty much confirm this, as, there is no other location where these two factors can be matched – Ballingham was wrong, for instance, as the pole route would have been on the other side of the line – although the distant higher ground of the Cotswold escarpment between Gloucester and Stroud, on the far side of the River Severn, seems a tad more prominent than I would have expected. CHRIS WALKER

This slide also came with no details on the mount and although clearly in the vicinity of Longhope, the growth of trees and bushes along the route in the years since these pictures were taken and the line was closed has again made pinning down the exact location difficult, whilst the white painted bungalow in the left background has defied attempts at finding it. However, I am fairly certain that this is a Down train heading for Hereford in 1964 and we are looking east across the valley, with Velthouse Lane running along somewhere behind the train or even behind the bungalow. The locomotive is a '41XX' Series 'Large Prairie' and the train is a typical three coach working, with a Hawksworth Brake Composite next to the engine. NPC

Although the main building at Longhope could justifiably be described as unprepossessing at best, the station nevertheless managed to maintain an air of attractive charm which certainly drew in the photographers. There is little to enable us to guess at a date here and the 'Mogul' is not unidentifiable but some time during the last months of operation in 1964 would again seem a fair bet. A solitary passenger almost hidden behind the porter on the right would appear to be the only custom for the Gloucester-bound train on this occasion, along with perhaps the photographer. The bicycle propped against the seat on the Down platform probably belonged to the signalman – one of Trevor Owen's views shows a moped parked at the same spot. NPC

LEFT: A closer view of the stone-built waiting shelter on the Up side, which, like that at Grange Court, had a gents toilets attached at the nearer end; in the Victorian age, ladies were often not provided for in the same way! The station site is now a private garden and this building survives converted for use as a summer house. NPC

BELOW: Collett Class '22XX' 0-6-0 No. 3242 can just be seen in the background, drawing in with the 12.38pm train to Hereford, as the Longhope signalman ambles along the platform with the single line token for the section to Mitcheldean Road. The exchange could have been effected in front of the box but he then would not have had the chance to pass the time of day briefly with the footplate crew, before the train went on its way again. JOHN RYAN

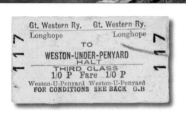

Gt. Western Ry.   Gt. Western Ry.
Longhope   Longhope
           TO
WESTON-UNDER-PENYARD
           HALT
        THIRD CLASS
    1/0 P Fare 1/0 P
Weston-U-Penyard Weston-U-Penyard
  FOR CONDITIONS SEE BACK G.B

BELOW: Longhope was photographed on the same day as Oakle Street and Blaisdon by Roy Denison, 3rd November 1962, the bright sunshine seemingly coming in between bouts of showery rain. The intention was clearly to record the stations themselves, with no interference from passing trains, and the viewpoint and the lighting clearly helped to show off Longhope's idyllic location to its very best. ROY DENISON

LEFT: The goods workings on the line were much less frequently photographed. However, on his visit of 3rd November 1962 Roy Denison captured Collett No. 2242 as it made its way through with a Hereford to Gloucester pick-up goods. A branch regular, it appears several times through these pages. ROY DENISON

RIGHT: A view of the station from the second carriage behind 'Large Prairie" No. 4115 as it threads a service to Gloucester over the level crossing and into the Up platform on 7th June 1962. NPC

BELOW: A circa 1962 view of No. 6304 arriving over the level crossing with a train for Gloucester, past a line of vans in the double-ended goods siding. Unlike regulars such as No. 2242 above, this is the only time within these pages that we shall encounter Gloucester Horton Road-based No. 6304, which was to spend its last five years in service working from 85B, up to its withdrawal in January 1964. New in December 1920, the outside steam pipes were fitted by BR at Swindon in January 1952. NPC

Ubiquitous No. 2242 strolls away from the smokey confines of Lea Line Tunnel with the 12.25pm from Gloucester to Hereford on 9th May 1964. The footplate crew were clearly aware of the photographer, the fireman also taking the chance for a breather on the coast downhill towards the next stop at Mitcheldean Road, half a mile away. NPC

BELOW: The first of a pair of summer 1964 views, showing Collett 0-6-0 No. 2287 setting off from Mitcheldean Road having slowed to exchange the single line staff with the signalman, walking back to his box on the left. Note the new BR vans at the front of the train, which is likely to be the Lydbrook goods, serving the cable works at Lydbrook Junction on the Ross-Monmouth Branch. In filthy condition, No. 2287 is sporting a Severn Tunnel Junction 86E shedplate on its smokebox door but had been transferred to Gloucester Horton Road 85B by the time of its withdrawal in May 1965. NPC

LEFT: Looking east through the station, as No. 2287 heads away towards Gloucester. NPC

LEFT: Winter sunlight brightens this view to The Lea from beneath the canopy of the main building on 7th March 1964 To save passengers using the Up side from having to walk any further than necessary, a carriage length of edging stones were left in place at the east end, so all anyone had to do was cross the line and climb the ramp but such practice all looks very unsafe now. TIM STEPHENS

ABOVE: Taken on the same day, the light dusting of snow would undoubtedly have made conditions on the platforms even more treacherous, albeit whilst serving to enhance this Christmas card-like panorama of the station for a 21st century audience. The leaden sky above The Lea carries a promise of more snow to come. TIM STEPHENS

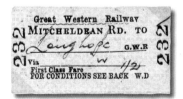

RIGHT: A sprinkling of passengers gather on the short section of the Up platform that still retained its edging stones, ready to board the 11.03am from Hereford to Gloucester, hauled by No. 6128, on 15th August 1964. The crew had already exchanged the staff with the signalman, who can be seen heading back to his box in the left background. JOHN RYAN

I love views with human interest and this shot of Mitcheldean Road station, with ex-GWR 'Mogul' No. 6364 disappearing off towards Weston-under-Penyard with the 9.48am train from Gloucester to Hereford is particularly delightful. Grandad may have just got off the train to be met by the children or he may have brought them here to watch a few trains passing through as closure – and the end of an era – loomed. Meanwhile, the station master and signalman have a chat before the latter heads back in to his box. No photograph of the original Mitcheldean Road station building has ever been seen but it is likely that it was in the same style as those that survived until the end at Longhope and Holme Lacy; the signal box dated from the addition of the Up platform in 1898. This view shows well the paraphernalia that went to make up a steam age railway station scene – the various signs and posters, including an enamelled GWR notice, the loaded parcels trolley and the token apparatus. The floral display on the Down platform was also a sight to behold. JOHN RYAN

ABOVE: Whilst motive power on the line was very varied, particularly on the 7.50am Swindon to Hereford service, which Richard Dagley-Morris tells me often had a Shrewsbury engine on the front, this slide is without doubt the most remarkable discovery to date – I never expected to find that a 'Jubilee' had featured on the line and it has rather surprised everyone else I've spoken to! From October 1961 to its withdrawal in November 1964, No. 45699 *Galatea* was a Shrewsbury based engine, so it was clearly conforming to the rule above but the very fact that the crew are posing for the sadly unknown photographer indicates that all concerned were very aware of the unusual nature of this particular working. No. 45699 is happily still with us, having been rescued from Barry scrapyard in 1980 and is now based at Carnforth. NPC

RIGHT: Gloucester Horton Road's ex-GWR 'Mogul' No. 6349 was clearly sporting a home-made smokebox door numberplate and other depot staff 'embellishments' to its front end steelwork when it was photographed heading light engine past the signal box in the summer of 1964. Transferred from Llanelly in September 1963, it was to be withdrawn in early August 1964. CHRIS WALKER

BELOW: A closer study of the Up side waiting shelter from a Down train. NPC

LEFT: Immediately after leaving Mitcheldean Road the line ran through a short but rather dramatic cutting, lined with stone buttress walls at the base. This 7th March 1964 view is looking towards Ross. TIM STEPHENS

ABOVE: A field level view of the line heading round from Mitcheldean Road and Lea Bailey Hill, in the right background, with No. 2242 coasting gently past towards the A40 overbridge with the 12.25pm train from Gloucester to Hereford on 9th May 1964. The low viewpoint clearly shows the downward gradient here, which extended all the way through Weston-under-Penyard and almost to Ross. NPC

RIGHT: One of the sections of line that I was unable to illustrate in the first edition of this volume was that on the other side of the A40 at Wharton Lodge – a gap that we can now fill. Taken on the same day as the previous picture, No. 4161 was working bunker first back to Gloucester with the 1.40pm from Hereford, through another length of cutting lined with stone buttress walls. The pine trees on the right formed a protective barrier on the western boundary of Wharton Lodge House and are still there today. The cutting, however, has gone, filled in to the level of the land either side. The stone-built overbridge in the background, which carried a farm access track, has also gone, although whether it was demolished or still lies buried beneath the infill I have been unable to ascertain. NPC

This view of Weston-under-Penyard Halt from the base of the embankment provides us with a rather more dramatic indication of its situation. On 3rd November 1962, Class '2XX' No. 2286 pauses with a train for Ross and Hereford. The locomotive had transferred from Machynlleth to Hereford about a month before this picture was taken. ROY DENISON

ABOVE: The fireman of No. 7815 *Fritwell Manor* leans out ready for the token exchange with the Ross signalman as they pass the box, to save him a walk down to the other end of the platform to effect the handover once the train had come to a halt. No. 7815 was withdrawn days before the line closed. NPC

BELOW: Roy Denison's visit to the line of 3rd November 1962 ended at Ross, where he took three pictures, one of which was this fine panorama of the eastern approaches and the engine shed, with an unidentified Collett 0-6-0 standing outside. In the foreground is the bay platform Starter signal for the Monmouth Branch, which was clearly still well maintained although had not been in use for nearly three years. ROY DENISON

RIGHT: 'Large Prairie No. 4135 throws up a plume of white steam as it heads smartly away with a service for Gloucester on 3rd November 1962. Note the centre coach of its train is still in the 1950s carmine and cream livery, a fairly unusual sight by this date. On the left, the weeds growing between the sleepers and the rust on the rails of the Monmouth bay mark the fact that nearly three years had passed since branch services had been withdrawn. ROY DENISON

LEFT: No. 7814 *Fringford Manor* arrives with the 14.38pm train from Hereford on 14th August 1964. The view provides useful detail of the underside of the canopy and the cast iron support columns. The station looks quiet for a Saturday, perhaps a sign that the withdrawal of passenger services was just ten weeks away. JOHN RYAN

RIGHT: More under canopy detail in this view of another 'Manor Class', No. 7815 *Fritwell Manor*, arriving with the 14.47pm train to Hereford, which photographer John Ryan will board to travel further on up the line. Ross was the only intermediate station on the route to be provided with a footbridge, a handsome affair with a covered roof, glazed windows and quite substantial for a station of this size. JOHN RYAN

There is much to study here in Roy Denison's third and final view of Ross-on-Wye, another panoramic shot which shows this delightful, rural market town station in all its glory. The 1st edition 25 inch Ordnance Survey of 1889 appears to show the the original station at Ross, opened on 1st June 1855, had an overall roof or train shed, which would have been typical of a broad gauge station of that period. However, no photographs of it or indeed of the railway here pre-1900 have ever been seen. The buildings seen here all dated from the station's reconstruction in 1892. The Up side shelter had a brick building behind it, the chimney of which can be seen jutting up above the roof, which housed waiting rooms and toilets, whilst the extensive facilities on the Down platform included a refreshments room. The station's name was simply Ross from opening up to 1933, when it became Ross-on-Wye, no doubt to better reflect its location as the local tourist industry became an ever more important part of the area's economy. ROY DENISON

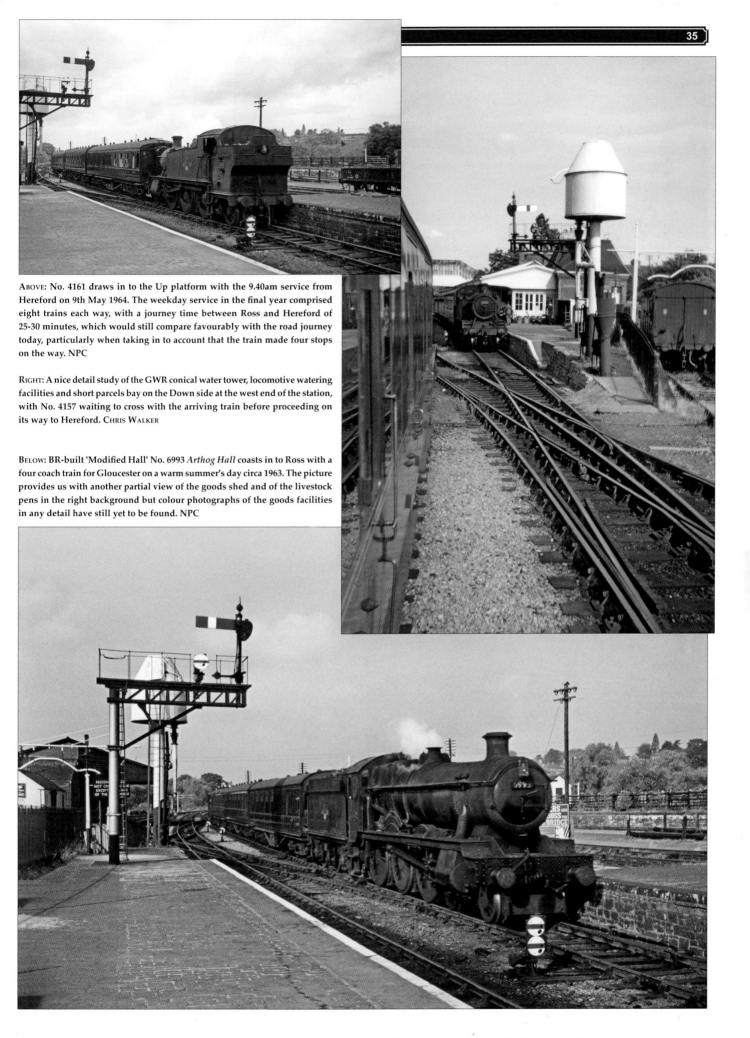

ABOVE: No. 4161 draws in to the Up platform with the 9.40am service from Hereford on 9th May 1964. The weekday service in the final year comprised eight trains each way, with a journey time between Ross and Hereford of 25-30 minutes, which would still compare favourably with the road journey today, particularly when taking in to account that the train made four stops on the way. NPC

RIGHT: A nice detail study of the GWR conical water tower, locomotive watering facilities and short parcels bay on the Down side at the west end of the station, with No. 4157 waiting to cross with the arriving train before proceeding on its way to Hereford. CHRIS WALKER

BELOW: BR-built 'Modified Hall' No. 6993 *Arthog Hall* coasts in to Ross with a four coach train for Gloucester on a warm summer's day circa 1963. The picture provides us with another partial view of the goods shed and of the livestock pens in the right background but colour photographs of the goods facilities in any detail have still yet to be found. NPC

LEFT: A close-up of the Down side waiting shelter circa 1963, with a lone lady passenger about to board a Hereford bound train. NPC

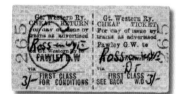

RIGHT: The Fawley signalman waits to greet and exchange tokens with the 16.48pm from Hereford, with No. 2286 at the head, on 14th August 1964 but there are no passengers waiting, apart from the photographer who was about to climb aboard. JOHN RYAN

LEFT: This service for Hereford in summer 1964 has just been given the 'off' and will shortly head in to the narrow confines of Fawley Tunnel in the middle distance; note how the line breasted a summit beneath the bridge and then drops on a shallow gradient towards the tunnel mouth. A Wickham maintenance trolley belonging to the local permanent way gang can be seen parked on the goods yard siding and note that the letter 'L' on the nameboard had lost its battle with gravity. CHRIS WALKER

A stunning view of the railway from above the western portal of Fawley Tunnel on 16th May 1964, with the line heading over Ballingham Bridge towards the station in the centre distance. The signal in the foreground is the Fawley Distant, which was permanently fixed at caution. TIM STEPHENS

To match his view of the line from above Fawley Tunnel, Tim Stephens also took this superb study of the small goods yard at Ballingham, looking from the stone bridge carrying the lane from Carey to Ballingham over the railway. Trees now occupy much of the site today, obscuring the view east. TIM STEPHENS

A young girl and her mother leave a Down train at Ballingham The bridge survives today, with the trackbed beyond for around 100 yards in the direction of Fawley now seemingly part of the garden for the private house that the station building has been converted to. NPC

Photographer John Ryan, having just alighted from the departing train, took this view of No. 7815 *Fringford Manor* as it made its way off round the curve towards Ballingham Tunnel on 14th August 1964. Having to make use of the time table to visit and photograph as many of the stations and halts as possible, it made for an interesting exercise planning where and when to get off and then be able to get back on again within a reasonable time. Ballingham village, which was and still is little more than a scattered collection of a few houses and farms, lay half a mile off to the north-east, with the equally small hamlet of Lower Pen-alt a little closer to the south-west but road transport was always going to erode the station's meagre ration of passengers and so it proved. JOHN RYAN

A view of the west end of Holme Lacy station building, from a Down train on its way to Hereford circa 1963. Although serving a slightly larger – and growing – community than Ballingham, Holme Lacy remained as built for its entire existence, surprising perhaps given that the isolated Mitcheldean Road station was rebuilt. The overbridge survives today but nothing of the station remains, its site remaining undeveloped but heavily overgrown. NPC

A detailed view of Holme Lacy station building's east elevation, as No. 4152 arrives with the 13.26pm from Hereford on 14th August 1964. I had originally thought that the bag prominent in the foreground here, which matched one also seen a little earlier on the platform at Fawley, was a mail sack – until John Ryan told me that it was actually his rucksack, which held a day's provisions, notebooks and pencils, time tables, his camera and anything else required to facilitate a day out riding and photographing the line! Now you know this, it can also be spotted in his views at Longhope and just creeping in to the bottom of the picture at Blaisdon. Note the corrugated iron goods lock-up shed behind the station building on the right. JOHN RYAN

ABOVE: A lovely view of the Hereford station's handsome frontage and the forecourt circa 1962, with a fine array of period motor cars on view. With assistance from Malcolm Bobbit, we can identify them as (left to right from the lamppost): A Ford Zodiac, a Hillman Minx and a Ford Prefect (with a Morris Traveller in front). In the right foreground is a Morris Eight Series II which, from the registration number, dates from circa 1936. Note the odd headlamps – that on the near side of the car looks the original, the off-side being chromed and more modern, whilst the bumper is missing, so perhaps the car had been in an accident. NPC

BELOW: The depot steam crane at Hereford no doubt had various uses but prime amongst them would have been for loading the ashes from locomotives in to wagons for removal. The crane, about which nothing else is known, is seen here on 26th June 1964 loading a steel mineral wagon with ash. H.W. ROBINSON/NPC

RIGHT: A short goods departs from the Up side yard via the through goods line running behind the Up platform, heading for the Ross and Gloucester line behind Collett 0-6-0 No. 2286 in August 1964. The locomotive is partially obscuring the signal box nameplate, Aylestone Hill, the lack of the words 'Signal Box' on the plate giving a clue as to its joint GWR/L&NWR origins. It was one of only nine built to the Joint Type 2 design, by the Railway Signal Company, fitted with a 62 lever Saxby & Farmer rocker frame and opened in July 1884. A replacement 69 lever GWR vertical tappet 5-bar frame was installed in June 1938. The box was renamed Hereford on 9th June 1973 and the frame reduced to 60 levers around the same time. A Kearns-Barker one control switch signalling panel was commissioned on 11th November 1984 to control Shelwick Junction, allowing the box there to be closed. Hereford box is still in operation today but was fitted with uPVC windows in the mid-2000s. CHRIS WALKER

LEFT: Photographed on the same day, No. 4157 runs round its three coach train in preparation for making the return journey to Gloucester. CHRIS WALKER

BELOW: Photographer Chris Walker photographed No. 4157 departing the station (page right) before returning to catch the next eastbound service, behind classmate No. 4161. Aylestone Hill signal box can be seen again in the background, with the bridge behind carrying the road from which the box took its name. The semaphore signals have gone, as have the carriage sidings running behind the box but the scene is otherwise still recognisable today. CHRIS WALKER

Arguably, this is the classic view at Hereford station, from the A465 Aylestone Hill overbridge, with No. 4157 departing bunker first for Gloucester. The station footbridge, partially seen in the left background, has been rebuilt to conform to modern disability requirements, so now has new lift towers either end and a new span, albeit to a similar design to that seen here. The Hawksworth coach in the carriage sidings on the right may well be part of another Ross/Gloucester line set, whilst the houses behind front on to Barrs Court Road, from which the station at first (and periodically afterwards) took its full name. The houses still remain but the pre-fab buildings of the school in the centre background have been rebuilt and now house Barrs Court Special School. CHRIS WALKER

Post closure views are rarely as satisfying as pictures taken when the lines were still open but these two excellent studies of St. Briavels station – so rarely photographed in any case – could not be omitted. They were taken in late summer 1964, with the vegetation already growing wild and the rails heavily rusted, despite the goods service having only been withdrawn at the beginning of that year. Looking towards Monmouth, they provide good detail of the buildings here, including the signal box by the level crossing. Very sadly, since the first edition was published, I have to record that the goods shed has been demolished. Both NPC

A visit to Paul Chancellor of Colour-Rail looking for pictures of the Midland lines for Volume 3 also produced this breathtaking, recently acquired view of the Wye Valley motor train heading away from Brockweir Halt circa 1955. Hauled by a pannier tank, the train comprises an ex-GWR Diagram A31 59ft 6ins auto trailer (converted from one of the steam rail motors in the number series 73-83 in 1934-35) and a Suburban Brake Third with driving compartment in the van end; both are in the unlined BR crimson livery of the early to mid 1950s, with the bright paintwork of the latter vehicle suggesting it had recently been outshopped. The view is looking from the Brockweir village side of the River Wye and the train is approaching the Tintern Home signal, the station being just out of sight around the curve. COLOUR-RAIL

ABOVE: Photographed from the footbridge, No. 6158 arrives at Chepstow with a two coach stopping train. New in 1933, the engine was at Severn Tunnel Junction shed from August 1961 to October 1963 (so the picture is within this date range), when it was transferred away to Aberdare, from where it was withdrawn in June 1964. There is a glimpse inside the signal box through the open window and plenty of traffic on view in the goods yard. NPC

BELOW: A nice study of the Down side shelter from a train in the Up platform circa 1962, with coaching stock also standing in the erstwhile Monmouth Branch platform. Sadly this fine Brunellian building was demolished in 1970. The lamppost was a recent installation, the older GWR lamps still featuring in the 1960 views. NPC

This view of Tutshill Halt, from a colour print rather than a slide, fills yet another gap in the first edition of this book. Taken on 14th April 1962 from the top of the cutting, ex-GWR '28XX' Class 2-8-0 No. 2857 trundles through heading back to South Wales with a long train of empty mineral wagons. Tutshill Halt had a short existence, being a late opening by the GWR, on 9th July 1934, whilst being served only by Wye Valley Branch trains, it closed with the service to Monmouth on 5th January 1959. Fortunately, over three years later, the sleeper-built platforms, shelters, lampposts and steps down each side were all still in place. No. 2857 had enjoyed a long career; built at Swindon Works in May 1918 and a resident of Aberdare shed at the date of this picture, the engine had just under a year left in traffic, being withdrawn from Neath Court Sart in late March 1963. NPC INSET: A Chepstow-Wye Valley Junction temporary works electric token. These 'temp sections' were in vogue in the 1950s/early '60s for major track and structure works. Here it was provided for the stages of the Chepstow Bridge re-building in 1961-62, which necessitated closure of one line whilst the other remained open for traffic. JOHN JENKIN COLLECTION

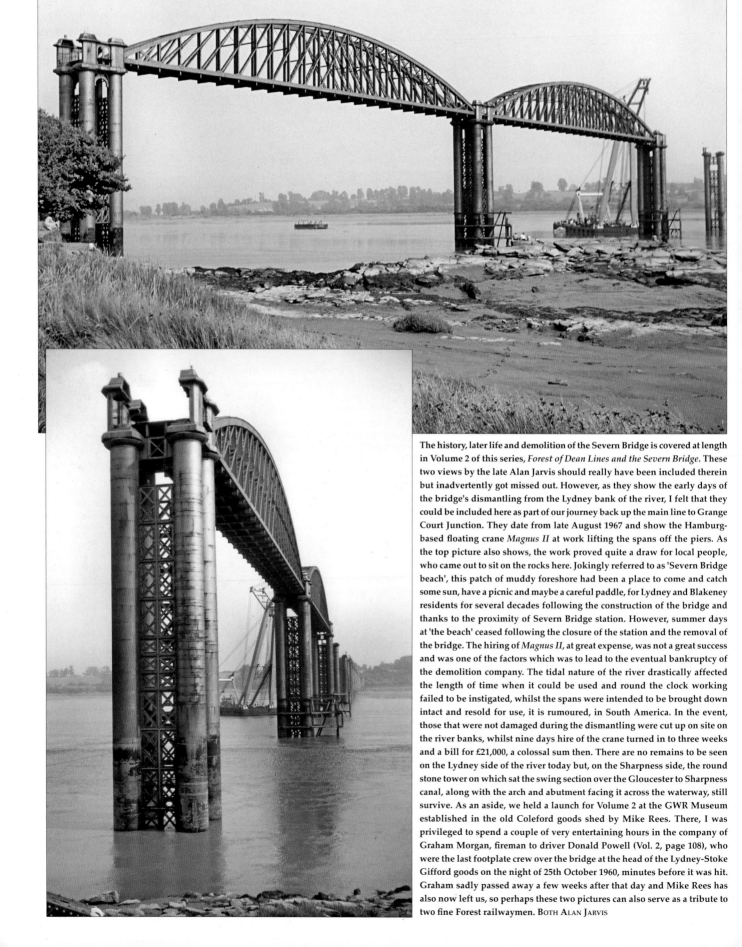

The history, later life and demolition of the Severn Bridge is covered at length in Volume 2 of this series, *Forest of Dean Lines and the Severn Bridge*. These two views by the late Alan Jarvis should really have been included therein but inadvertently got missed out. However, as they show the early days of the bridge's dismantling from the Lydney bank of the river, I felt that they could be included here as part of our journey back up the main line to Grange Court Junction. They date from late August 1967 and show the Hamburg-based floating crane *Magnus II* at work lifting the spans off the piers. As the top picture also shows, the work proved quite a draw for local people, who came out to sit on the rocks here. Jokingly referred to as 'Severn Bridge beach', this patch of muddy foreshore had been a place to come and catch some sun, have a picnic and maybe a careful paddle, for Lydney and Blakeney residents for several decades following the construction of the bridge and thanks to the proximity of Severn Bridge station. However, summer days at 'the beach' ceased following the closure of the station and the removal of the bridge. The hiring of *Magnus II*, at great expense, was not a great success and was one of the factors which was to lead to the eventual bankruptcy of the demolition company. The tidal nature of the river drastically affected the length of time when it could be used and round the clock working failed to be instigated, whilst the spans were intended to be brought down intact and resold for use, it is rumoured, in South America. In the event, those that were not damaged during the dismantling were cut up on site on the river banks, whilst nine days hire of the crane turned in to three weeks and a bill for £21,000, a colossal sum then. There are no remains to be seen on the Lydney side of the river today but, on the Sharpness side, the round stone tower on which sat the swing section over the Gloucester to Sharpness canal, along with the arch and abutment facing it across the waterway, still survive. As an aside, we held a launch for Volume 2 at the GWR Museum established in the old Coleford goods shed by Mike Rees. There, I was privileged to spend a couple of very entertaining hours in the company of Graham Morgan, fireman to driver Donald Powell (Vol. 2, page 108), who were the last footplate crew over the bridge at the head of the Lydney-Stoke Gifford goods on the night of 25th October 1960, minutes before it was hit. Graham sadly passed away a few weeks after that day and Mike Rees has also now left us, so perhaps these two pictures can also serve as a tribute to two fine Forest railwaymen. BOTH ALAN JARVIS